Art Masterpieces of
FLORENCE

Designed and Produced by

TED SMART

and

DAVID GIBBON

CRESCENT

INTRODUCTION

From the Middle Ages Florence has been an important centre of art, science and political thought. Her history, however, dates back to c. 187 BC, when the Roman town of Florentia was built at the foot of a hill on which stood the Etruscan town of Faesulae, now known as Fiesole. The name, Florentia, meaning 'flourishing town', was probably chosen as an augury and, indeed, the town did flourish and become an important centre, as roads from east to west and north to south, along the Arno Valley, were extended through the city, although commerce, craftsmanship and an abundant supply of water were also contributory factors to her growth.

In the years that followed, invasion by the Goths, and later by the Byzantines and Lombards, reduced the Roman amphitheatre, temples, baths and other buildings to piles of rubble. It was the great Charlemagne, who visited the city no less than three times, to whom legend accords responsibility for the reconstruction of Florence in the 8th century. The medieval city was built on a level from four to ten feet above the ancient remains and it included many fine churches.

In 1052 Florence, together with the rest of Tuscany passed into the hands of Countess Matilda and, under her influence, progressed towards political and administrative autonomy. The city, however, had grave internal problems in the form of conflicts between the Guelphs and the Ghibellines. The Florentine people, the Guelphs, were loyal to the Popes, and the Ghibellines to the Emperors. As one party won so it would exile the other, who would lose no time in seeking assistance from outside in order to recover power. It was during this time that an exiled Ghibelline from Florence, Dante Alighieri, chose the more vulgar speech of Tuscany in which to write his epic work 'The Divine Comedy', and in so doing made Tuscan the literary language of Sicily.

In 1250 the city was proclaimed a republic and after ten years of Guelph supremacy Florence became not only one of the chief cites of Italy but one of the most influential in civilized Europe.

From 1434 her history was intertwined with the rich and powerful Medicis – a family of bankers. Cosimo de' Medici was a great benefactor of literature and the arts and a friend of other Italian and European rulers. He was succeeded by his son Piero the Gouty, whose reign was brief and undistinguished. Lorenzo the Magnificent, who followed Piero, was a poet of considerable talent and, like his grandfather, a wise politician and a patron of the arts. It was under his rule that Florence was adorned with great artistic works and became the centre of European culture. His son Giovanni became Pope Leo X and another Medici, Francesco I, was responsible for founding the world famous Uffizi Gallery. Ferdinand I, his brother, under whom Florence attained even greater heights of power and prosperity, was next to rule but his successors, alas, were responsible for the city's decline and the eventual transference of power to the House of Lorraine.

Francesco was the Lorraine's first Duke of Tuscany. He was, however, married to Maria Teresa of Austria and preferred to live in Vienna where, in 1745, he received the crown of the Hapsburg Empire. From 1765-1790, Tuscany came under the competent rule of Pietro Leopoldo but he too was summoned to assume the crown of Austria. His son Ferdinand III was left to govern but he was weak and before long he was expelled by French forces and the Duchy was ruled successively by Ludovico I of Parma and Elisa Baciocchi, the sister of Napoleon. With the death of the French Emperor, Ferdinand III returned to Tuscany to regain his dukedom and for a time the region enjoyed relative peace under him and his son Leopold II.

However, during a wave of nationalism in the middle of the nineteenth century, Leopold II was driven out, and in 1860 Tuscany proclaimed itself part of the kingdom of Italy – of which Florence became the capital from 1865-1871.

Perhaps the next most significant happening in the history of Florence was during the summer of 1944. World War II had reduced much of the Tuscany coast to a battlefield. Sadly for Florence German troops blew up all her bridges except the Ponte Vecchio, as well as many of the medieval buildings along the Arno River. After they had retreated rebuilding began in earnest.

Another tragedy occurred in 1966 when terrible floods, believed to be worse than those of 1333 and 1557, caused immense and costly damage, both to buildings and to art treasures. In some places water rose to a depth of nearly twenty feet, leaving everywhere deposits of mud and debris, as well as oil from central heating systems. The Uffizi Gallery and the Pitti Palace escaped but many churches and their contents suffered badly. International aid poured into the city and this, together with the rugged determination of the Florentines, enabled much of the damage to be rectified. Restoration still continues but all the museums and monuments have now reopened – to be admired by countless visitors from all over the world.

In her fine buildings Florence displays the genius of architects like Brunelleschi, Giotto, Alberti and Buonotalenti, and inside them may be seen the outstanding work of such masters as Ghirlandaio, Titian, Botticelli, Fra Angelico, Michelangelo and Leonardo da Vinci.

The whole of Florence may fairly be described as one magnificent treasure house. The Uffizi Gallery has collections of incalculable value which include major works from all the Italian and other European Schools. The Pitti Palace, built in the middle of the fifteenth century, has over five hundred paintings beautifully displayed and the Academy contains Michelangelo's renowned sculpture 'David' as just one of its exhibits.

The rest of Florence's great buildings are too numerous to describe fully in the space available here. Only a visit to this unique city can fully reveal the splendour of her heritage or, failing that, a book such as this, which lays before the reader many of the glories of Florence.

The magnificent statue of David, in the Gallery of the Academy *left*, is the work of **Michelangelo** Buonarroti (c. 1475-1564).

The historic buildings of the beautiful city of Florence cluster around the Cathedral of Santa Maria del Fiore, the third largest church in the world, and although work began on the cathedral in 1296, it was not completed until the end of the 19th century. Towering regally over the red-tiled roofs *above* is the cupola, Brunelleschi's masterpiece, whilst *above right* the magnificent façade, faced with coloured marble, blends harmoniously with the Baptistry *far right*. Built on the site of an old, early Christian Basilica, the octagonal plan of the Baptistry, with geometric marble patterns, is an outstanding example of Romanesque architecture. Of the three gilt-bronze doors, the most splendid is the East door, known as the Gate of Paradise. This masterpiece of Renaissance art represents, in ten panels, scenes from the Old Testament, and took Lorenzo **Ghiberti** (c. 1378-1455), with the help of his sons, twenty seven years to complete.

The scene of the city's major historical events, the Piazza Della Signoria *right*, is dominated by the Palazzo Vecchio with its elegant tower and mullioned windows.

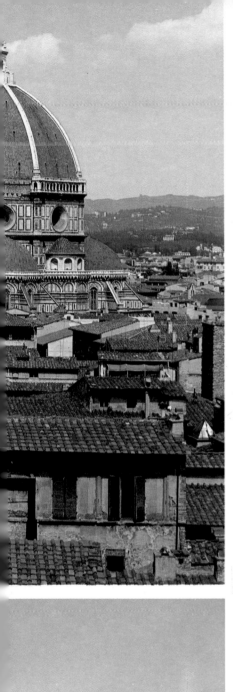

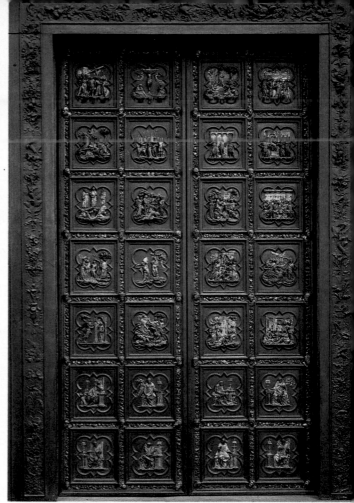

The East door of the Baptistry is illustrated *above,* revealing the extent of Ghiberti's craftsmanship and *right* is shown in detail the panel representing the meeting between Solomon and the Queen of Sheba.

Also the work of **Ghiberti,** the North door *above right* is similar to that of Pisano's South door, in that both are divided into twenty-eight panels. Executed in 1425, with the help of some of his pupils who included Donatello and Uccello, the panels depict scenes from the New Testament, Doctors of the Church and the lives of the Evangelists.

Situated in the last chapel of the left transept of the Santa Maria del Fiore Cathedral is **Michelangelo's** emotive study, the 'Pietà' *left.* It is thought that the artist intended to have the sculpture placed on his own tomb, but the work was unfinished at the time of his death and completed by Tiberio Calcagni, who added the figure of Mary Magdalene. Nevertheless, the dramatic, rhythmic lines created by the continuous intertwining of the bodies, convey the deep sense of emotion in the theme of the 'Descent from the Cross'.

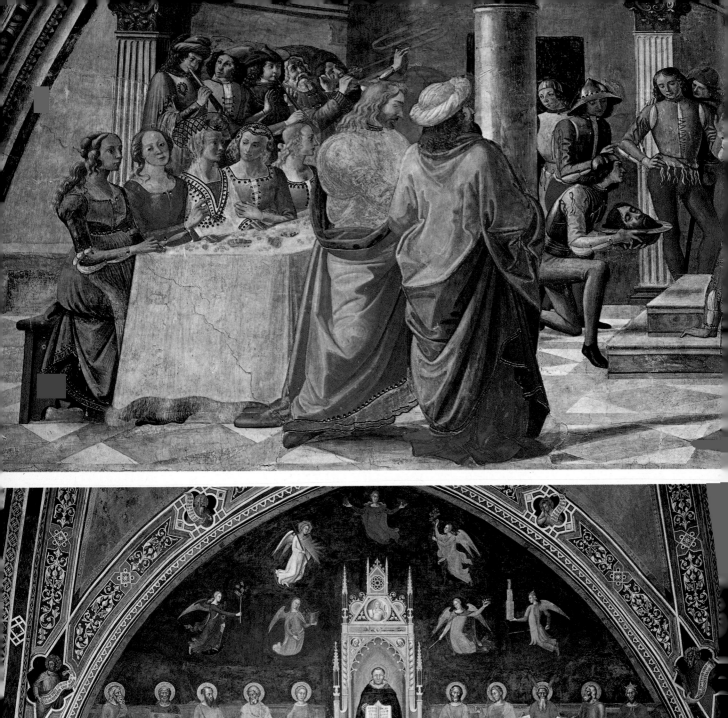

In the church of Santa Maria Novella, the apse of the main chapel is covered with a series of frescoes including the detail *above left* from 'Herod's Feast and the Dance of Salome' by Domenico **Ghirlandaio** (c. 1449-1494): featured in the Spanish chapel is 'The Triumph of St Thomas Aquinas' *left* by **Andrea da Firenze** (c. 1337-1377).

Within the Church of Santa Croce are many outstanding works of art, amongst them the magnificent Tomb of Michelangelo, and the painting *above*, 'The Doubting Thomas' by Giorgio **Vasari** (c. 1511-1574).

The Laurentian Library *above*, designed by **Michelangelo** for Pope Clement VII, houses a rare collection of priceless manuscripts, including the famous Virgil of the 4th or 5th centuries, and about 100 codices of Dante.

The Brancacci chapel, within the Carmine Church, contains a cycle of frescoes begun in 1424–5 by **Masolino** da Panicale (c. 1384–1447) and completed by his pupil, **Masaccio** (c. 1401–1428), who painted 'The Expulsion of Adam and Eve from Paradise' *above right*. Also included in the fifteen frescoes are 'The Temptation of Adam and Eve' *above far right* and 'St Peter raises Tabitha from the Dead' *right*, executed conjointly by Masolino and Masaccio.

The Museum of San Marco is housed in an ancient 13th century convent, on the site of an old monastery of the Vallombrosian monks. Rebuilt in 1437, by Michelozzo, to the order of Cosimo the Elder, the Convent was taken over by the Dominican Order and **Fra Angelico** (Guido di Pietro) (about 1400–1455), with the help of a number of assistants, was responsible for the decoration of the cells and common rooms.

After the suppression of the monastic order, in 1866, the Convent was converted to a museum and devoted to Fra Angelico, who adopted the name of Fra Giovanni da Fiesole when he became a Dominican monk, some time between 1420 and 1422. The early Renaissance Florentine style of this deeply religious artist reveals his innate gentleness and sensitivity, and because of his angelic virtues, gave rise, after his death, to the name of Angelico.

The compassionate compositions, by Fra Angelico, illustrated on these pages, sombre in both theme and colour, portray with deep intensity the sufferings of Christ.

'Christ Mocked' is shown *above left*, 'The Crucifixion' *below left*, 'The Descent from the Cross' *right* and *below* 'Christ at the Gates of Hell'.

These further works exemplify Angelico's mastery. The detail *right* depicts the grieving Madonna 'Lamenting the Dead Christ', and the sublime facial expressions are indicative of the artist's deep emotional intensity.

Throughout his life Angelico combined the pious monastic life with continued activity as a painter, and although the majority of his work consists of the murals executed in the Convent of San Marco, he also worked in Rome, decorating the chapel of Pope Nicholas V, in the Vatican.

On his return to Florence, he was responsible for producing a cycle of thirty-five paintings for the door of a silver chest, which includes the familiar theme of 'The Last Supper' illustrated *above*, and *left* is shown 'Judas receiving Payment' for his betrayal of Christ. On the first floor of the Convent can be seen the old Dominican cells with the frescoes painted, for the most part, by Angelico and his pupils; and in the Prior's Quarters is sited the double cell, numbered 32-33, which is believed to be the one occupied by Angelico during his attachment to the Convent.

Within the Pilgrims' Hostel, which is sited to the right of the San Marco Museum entrance, are numerous paintings on wood which reveal Fra Angelico's development as an artist. Amongst the finest is 'The Last Judgement', details of which are shown *above, left and overleaf.*

The upper section *left* depicts Christ enthroned, surrounded by a heavenly host of angels, pronouncing his final judgement on mankind. The right-hand section, illustrated *overleaf* portrays the condemned descending into hell's inferno, whilst the left-hand section, pictured *above*, denotes the righteous joining with the angels in a jubilant dance.

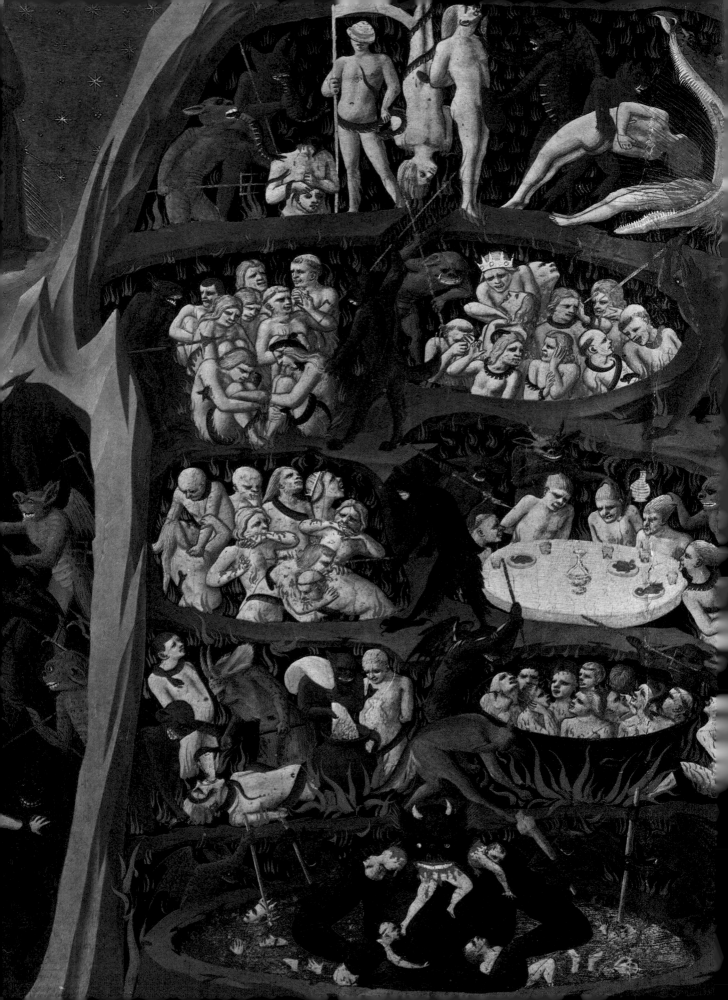

Leading from a small door off the hall on the first floor of the Palazzo Vecchio, also known as the Palazzo della Signoria or del Popolo, is the Study of Francesco I, exquisitely decorated by Giorgio **Vasari** (c. 1511-1574), and known as 'Il Tesoretto' (the Little Treasury), as it originally served as the Duke's strong-room.

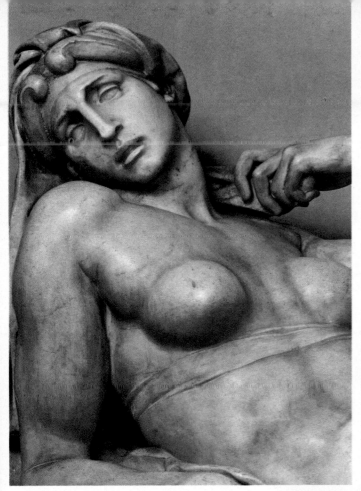

The Gallery of the Academy contains not
only a superb picture gallery, but also some of
Michelangelo's most important sculptures.
The 'Palestrina Pietà' *left*, although unfinished,
remains one of the artist's most significant
and moving works; the barely outlined faces
conveying pathos and anguish in this scene
of great drama.

Behind the Church of San Lorenzo are the
magnificent Medici Chapels, which can also
be reached from the interior of the Church.
In the New Sacristy, so called to distinguish it
from the Old Sacristy (the work of
Brunelleschi), are the tombs of the Medici
princes, the great rulers of Florence. Begun by
Michelangelo in 1520 and completed by
Vasari in 1557 the spacious interior is linked
by pilaster strips and blind windows, and the
emphasised outlines of 'pietra serena'.

The beautifully sculpted head of Giuliano,
Duke of Nemours, by Michelangelo, is
illustrated *right* and adorning the sarcophagus
beneath the sculpture are two figures
representing Day and Night, a detail of which
is shown *above right*. Michelangelo has
continued the theme on the sarcophagus of
the tomb of Lorenzo, Duke of Urbino, with
the figures denoting Dawn and Dusk, a detail
of which is shown *above*.

The Museum of the Opera del Duomo, at the rear of the Cathedral, contains relics from the Cathedral, the Baptistry and the Campanile and architectural remains from earlier buildings on the site. In the 'Room of the Choir Galleries' can be seen many important sculptures, including **Donatello**'s (c. 1386–1466) 'Jeremiah' *left*.

Within the 'Room of the Panels' are some of the panels carved by Andrea **Pisano** (c. 1270-90-1348-9) for the Campanile. The carving *below* represents the art of building and *below left* the medical practitioner. Also incorporated is the panel *above*, portraying the poet Orpheus and *above left* the pupils receiving instruction in Latin grammar.

The origins of the Church of San Lorenzo can be traced as far back as AD 393 when it was consecrated by St Ambroso, Bishop of Milan. The Church has undergone several major transformations, having been rebuilt in the Romanesque style in the 11th century, and later altered by Brunelleschi at the request of the Medici family, first in 1419 and again between 1442 and 1446. It was finally completed by Antonio Manetti, in 1460, except for the reconstruction of the façade, which was to have been carried out by Michelangelo. Michelangelo did, however, add the Laurentian Library and the New Sacristy, in the right arm of the transcept, which complements Brunelleschi's Old Sacristy; the latter being sited in the left arm.

In the centre aisle, on each side of the altar, are two pulpits executed by **Donatello** with the aid of his pupils, and which date from about 1460. Constructed of bronze and wood the pulpits, the exquisite detailing of which can be seen *above*, show the artists' superb craftsmanship and depict scenes from the 'Passion of Christ'. The panel *above right* portrays the emotional scene of 'Christ's Descent from the Cross' and illustrated *left* is 'Christ brought before Pilate'.

The magnificent Silver Reredos in the Museum of the Opera del Duomo is a superb example of Florentine gold-smiths' art of the 14th and 15th centuries. The intricate detailing on the altar screen depicts scenes from the life of St John the Baptist and *below* is illustrated a section of the screen portraying the meeting between Christ and the Prophet.

Construction on the famous Uffizi Palace *far right* began in 1560, to the plan of Giorgio **Vasari** (c. 1511–1574), for Cosimo I de' Medici. The original idea of the building was to provide administrative headquarters for Florence, but after the death of Cosimo, the offices were sited in the Palazzo Vecchio and the new Grand Duke was able, therefore, to utilize the Uffizi for the Medici art collections; so began the magnificent Gallery which now contains the greatest of Italian treasures as well as foreign art.

The whole building, which extends from the Arno River to the Palazzo Vecchio, is of local grey stone on white plaster and the famous 'Vasariano' corridor links the Gallery to the Pitti Palace.

The marble-floored 'Third Corridor' *above* is lined with beautiful tapestries, and sculptures of the 3rd and 4th centuries BC.

Commencing the Gallery's impressive collection of paintings, illustrated here and on the following eighteen pages are:–

'Madonna and Child with Angels and Prophets' *right*, by **Cimabue** (Cenni di Pepi) (before 1251–1302), an important work by this great Tuscan painter. 'Madonna and Child with Angels and Saints' *left*, by **Giotto** (di Bondone) (about 1267–1337) was originally painted for the High Altar of the Ognissanti Church.

One of the most sensitive exponents of Gothic art, Simone **Martini** (c. 1284-1344), did much to spread the influence of Sienese painting, and his work is imbued with pure, harmonious colour and a gracefulness of line. The triptych *above left*, 'The Annunciation' was painted in collaboration with his brother-in-law, Lippo **Memmi** (c. 1285-1361), for the Cathedral of Siena.

Gentile da Fabriano (G. di Nicolo di Giovanni Massi) (c. 1370-1450) executed the altarpiece, 'Adoration of the Magi', a detail of which is shown *left*, for the Strozzi Chapel in Santa Trinità, Florence. His work exemplifies the splendour of the Florid International Gothic style and this magnificent example is considered to be the artist's masterpiece.

The 'Coronation of the Virgin' *above* further illustrates the outstanding qualities of the art of **Fra Angelico**. Painted for the main Florentine Hospital of Santa Maria Nuova, the composition reveals his deep mysticism and combines both Gothic and Renaissance characteristics.

The 'Baptism of Christ' *left*, although attributed to the great sculptor Andrea del **Verrochio** (c. 1435-1488), reveals, as in much of his painting, the collaboration of other artists. It is believed that Leonardo, when an apprentice to Verrochio, contributed the angel in profile and the majority of the landscape.

The portraits of 'Federigo di Montefeltro' *below* and his wife 'Battista Sforza' *above* are the work of **Piero della Francesca** (c. 1420-1492) and denote the subtle and disciplined art of this important Italian Renaissance artist.

'The Ascension' *right* is part of a triptych by the first Renaissance artist of northern Italy, Andrea **Mantegna** (c. 1431?-1506); the other two panels depicting 'The Adoration of the Magi' and 'Circumcision'.

One of the greatest exponents of early
Florentine Renaissance art, Sandro **Botticelli**
(c. 1445-1510), trained under Fra Filippo
Lippi and by 1470 had established his own
atelier in Florence. Patronised by the
powerful Medici family, Botticelli's career was
highly successful and financially rewarding.
Included in the Gallery's extensive collection
of his paintings is the world-famous 'Birth of
Venus' *left*, which like 'Primavera' ('Allegory
of Spring') *above left*, embodies the spirit of the
renascent era. Botticelli painted 'Adoration of
the Kings' *above* for the Lami Chapel in Santa
Maria Novella, Florence, and several notable
members of the Medici family are depicted in
the composition, including Lorenzo the
Magnificent and Cosimo the Elder.

Pietro **Perugino** (c. 1450-1523) is noted for
his religious paintings and 'Madonna and
Child between St John the Baptist and St
Sebastian' *right* is a typical example of the
artist's work.

'The Annuciation' *right* and the unfinished painting of 'The Adoration of the Magi' *above right* are the work of **Leonardo** da Vinci (c. 1452-1519), a man of genius who excelled not only in the field of painting, developing his masterly technique of a superb atmospheric blending of light and shade, known as 'sfumato', but also in the spheres of sculpture, architecture and engineering. His drawings show his acute perception of the anatomy of the human body, whilst his scientific explorations reveal the brilliance that was centuries ahead of his time.

Luca **Signorelli** (c. 1445/50-1523), a Renaissance painter primarily known for his nudes and innovative compositional inventiveness, was strongly influenced by Florentine naturalism and in particular by the Pollaiuoli brothers. 'The Crucifix and Saints' *above*, portraying the SS Jerome, Francis and John the Baptist, the Blessed Colombini and Mary Magdalene, was painted in collaboration with **Perugino**.

Fra Filippo **Lippi** (c. 1406-1469) joined the Carmelite Order, in 1421, at Sta Maria del Carmine in Florence during the time that Masaccio was working on the frescoes in the Brancacci Chapel and his early work shows the influence of this outstanding artist. A highly gifted painter, Lippi also spent a considerable amount of time in Prato where he was responsible for the decoration of the Cathedral choir, and it was during this period that he was released from his vows in order to marry Lucrezia Buti, who gave birth to a son, Filippino, in 1457.

Included in the Gallery's wide collection of his paintings are the three superb examples illustrated on these pages.

'Madonna and Child with Two Angels' *left* is a particularly delightful study, enhanced by the gentle, ethereal beauty of the Madonna and typical of Renaissance art of the period, whilst the 'Adoration of the Infant Jesus with St Hilarius' *right* and 'Coronation of the Virgin' *above* reveal Lippi's intricate detailing and splendid use of colour.

Michelangelo Buonarroti (c. 1475-1564), like Leonardo, was one of the greatest and most versatile artists of the Renaissance, whose scope encompassed sculpture, painting, architecture and poetry. The magnificent 'Doni Tondo' *left* of 'The Holy Family' was painted on the occasion of the marriage between Agnolo Doni and Maddalena Strozzi.

'Rest on the Flight into Egypt' *right* is an early work by Antonio Allegri **Correggio** (c. 1494-1534) a Renaissance artist of the Parma school. Influenced by Raphael and Michelangelo, Correggio's paintings are remarkable for his harmonious use of colour and unified compositions.

The work of Lorenzo **Lotto** (c. 1480-1556) is characterised by his perceptive portraiture and mystical paintings of religious subjects. 'A Holy Conversation' *below* is a mature composition and depicts the Holy Family with the Saints Jerome and Anne.

One of the first of **Raphael** Santi's (c. 1483–1520) famed series of Madonna altarpanels 'The Madonna of the Goldfinch' is illustrated *left* and reveals his growing mastery of Leonardo's innovative 'sfumato' technique. The son of the painter Giovanni Santi, Raphael's early apprenticeship was to the Perugino, from where he moved first to Siena and then on to Florence, studying the works of the masters of the early Renaissance and Michelangelo and Leonardo. Ranked amongst the greatest of the Italian High Renaissance artists, Raphael is admired for his graceful compositions and skilful application of the art of perspective.

'Portrait of Leo X with the Cardinals Giulio de' Medici and Luigi de' Rossi' *above* is one of his later works and displays the formal grandeur and rich attire of the powerful church hierarchy.

Rosso Fiorentino (Giovanni Battista di Jacopo) (c. 1495-1540) was one of the founders of the Fontainebleau school, and his most highly regarded work is considered to be the decoration of the Galerie François I at the palace of Fontainebleau. 'A Putto Musician' *above* is a delightful painting by this influential artist and denotes the emotionalism of the Mannerist style.

Agnolo **Bronzino** (c. 1503–1572), a noted painter of the sophisticated Florentine Mannerist style, is particularly renowned for his portraiture which displays the impersonal, reserved poses favoured by the Medici, by whom he was employed as Court Painter. Initially influenced by Pontormo and to some extent by Michelangelo, he created his own precise style, developing a rich use of colour and high degree of finish. One of a pair of panel portraits 'Lucrezia Panciatichi' *right* is a companion study to that of her husband Bartolomeo, and illustrated *left* is 'Portrait of a Princess of the Medici family'.

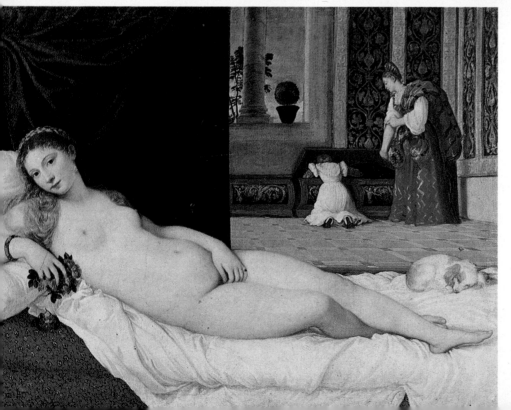

Influential in the development of Baroque painting, **Caravaggio** (Michelangelo Merisi) (c. 1573–1610), used the highly contrasted effects of light and shadow, known as tenebrism, to add drama to the realism of his paintings. 'The Youthful Bacchus' *above left* is an early composition by the artist, whose work was both revolutionary and original.

Generally regarded as the greatest German Renaissance artist, Albrecht **Dürer** (c. 1471–1528), was also an accomplished printmaker. 'Madonna and Child' *above* is one of his many paintings on religious themes.

'Flora' *right* and 'The Urbino Venus' *left* are indicative of the mastery of **Titian** (Tiziano Vecellio) (c. 1488/90–1576), whose skill in oil painting and brilliant use of colour place him among the finest artists of the Renaissance, and one of the outstanding figures of Western art.

The magnificent Pitti Palace was built to the plan of **Brunelleschi** by Luca **Pancelli** in 1458, for the Florentine banker Luca Pitti, who jealously challenged the supremacy of the Medici. Condemned to death for his actions, he was, however, reprieved and the Palace was purchased by Cosimo I.

Within the Palace is the splendid Palatine Gallery, housing a large collection of works of art, including 'The Young Bacchus' *right*, the work of Guido **Reni** (c. 1575-1642). The collection was started by Cosimo II, in 1620, and constantly enlarged by the Medici family and later by the House of Lorraine.

The exquisite Room of the Saturn *above*, named after the frescoes on the ceiling, executed by Ciro **Ferri** (c. 1634-1689), contains works by many outstanding artists, including Raphael, Perugino and Andrea del Sarto.

The Green Room *left*, noted for its superb Gobelin tapestries depicting Stories of Esther, is one of a suite of rooms, the former royal apartments, which were once reserved for the use of the Kings of Italy.

The paintings illustrated on these pages are further exhibits from the Uffizi Gallery.

'Madonna Enthroned between two Angels' *left* is an outstanding example of the work of the Flemish artist Hans **Memling** (c. 1430/35-1494), the leading painter of the Bruges school.

'Portrait of Marie Zefferina of France' *above*, the daughter of Louis XV, is characteristic of the style of the artist, Jean-Marc **Nattier** (c. 1685-1766), a celebrated portraitist of the period and particularly noted for his studies of court ladies in classical dress.

Formerly attributed to Holbein the impressive full-length portrait of 'François I of France' *right* is by François **Clouet** (c. 1515/20-1572), an eminent painter of the Valois Court.

Included in the Palatine Gallery's collection of art masterpieces are **Titian**'s 'Maddalena' *above*, and the 'Madonna of the Conception' *right* which denotes the depth of feeling and superb craftsmanship of the great Venetian Mannerist Painter Jacopo **Tintoretto** (c. 1518-1594). Tintoretto received a vast number of commissions, including the re-decoration of the Palace of the Doge, which he executed in collaboration with Veronese, after the earlier frescoes had been destroyed in the fire of 1577. An indefatigable worker, he maintained a large workshop where he was assisted by his daughter, Marietta and his sons Mario and Domenico.

The soft and gentle art of **Raphael** is further exemplified by the beautiful study of 'Madonna of the Grand Duke' *left*, displayed in the Palatine Gallery's Room of Saturn and by 'The Woman with a Veil' *above*, considered to be a portrait of the Fornarina and exhibited in the Room of Jupiter.

Within the Palatine Gallery is a room devoted to the allegorical paintings of Baldassare Franceschini **Volterrano** (c. 1611–1689), and his canvas depicting 'The Joke of the Parish Priest, Arlotto' is illustrated *left*.

'Judith and Holofernes' *right* is displayed in the Room of the Education of Jupiter. The work of Cristofani **Allori** (c. 1577–1621), a painter of the late Florentine Mannerist school, the composition is considered to be the artist's masterpiece.

The romantic landscape paintings of Salvator **Rosa** (c. 1615–1673) exerted a profound influence on 18th century English nature painters. The graceful accomplishments of this skilled artist encompassed those of poetry, music and acting: a gifted etcher, Rosa was also successful in producing a number of prints. 'The Broken Bridge' *above* is a superb example of his work.

The majority of the works of Bartolomé Esteban **Murillo** (c. 1618–1682) consist largely of religious themes and 'Madonna and Child' *left*, displayed in the Palatine Gallery's Room of Mars, is an exquisite example of his artistry.

The Room of the Iliad, with its splendidly decorated ceiling, contains the portrait of 'Waldemar Christian of Denmark' *right*, by the Flemish portrait and figure painter Justus **Sustermans** (c. 1597–1681), who spent the majority of his working life in Florence.

'The Consequences of War' *above* is one of the many mythological compositions by Peter Paul **Rubens** (c. 1577–1640); characteristic of the artist's dynamic energy, it embodies the sensuous exuberance of Baroque art, of which Rubens is considered to be the chief exponent.

Further paintings from the Gallery of the Pitti Palace are illustrated on this page.

'Madonna and Child' *above left* is the work of Carlo **Dolci** (c. 1616-1681) and characteristic of the artist's devotional paintings, executed with tender beauty and subtle colouring. A popular painter of his period, Dolci remained in Tuscany where he developed his style in the local Florentine Baroque tradition.

The portrait of 'Eleonora de' Medici' *above* is indicative of the ornate, grandiose style of the celebrated portraitist Frans **Pourbus** (c. 1569-1622). Employed at the Court of Mantua, Pourbus produced many studies of the nobility, including the Medici family and his paintings display the exquisite, ostentatious clothes of the era.

'The Three Fates' *left* is by Cecchino **Salviati** (Francesco de' Rossi) (c. 1510-1563), a pupil of Andrea del Sarto and one of the foremost Mannerist fresco painters of the Florentine-Roman school. This talented artist undertook a variety of ecclesiastical commissions, which he executed in Rome, Florence, Bologna and Venice, and among his most noteworthy frescoes are those painted for the Sala delle Udienza in the Palazzo Vecchio.

The intricately detailed composition *right*, 'The Golden Age', is the work of Jacopo **Zucchi** (c. 1541-1589/90), which is exhibited in the Uffizi Gallery.

Also included in the collection at the Pitti Palace are the following paintings:–

'Portrait of Musicians' *left* by Antonio Domenico **Gabbiani** (c. 1652–1726) who worked with Sustermans at his studio in Venice, and on his return to Florence established a highly successful Academy.

'A View of the Coast of Naples from the Sea' *above right* and 'The Convent of S. Paolo at Albano' *centre right* are both fine works by the artist and draughtsman, Gaspar van **Wittel** (c. 1653–1736), who was known in Italy as **Vanvitelli**.

'Naval Battle' *bottom right* is the work of Willem van de **Velde**, a noted painter of marine subjects.

Among the exhibits in the Museum Firenze Com'era, which houses a collection of engravings and drawings showing the development of Florence throughout the ages is the painting *below* depicting the 'Piazza Santa Croce during a Carnival' by Giovanni **Signorini** (c. 1450–1523).

Within the Medici–Riccardi Palace, the official residence of the Medici up to the time of Cosimo I, is displayed the beautifully detailed painting *below*, 'Voyage of the Three Kings', the work of Benozzo **Gozzoli** (c. 1420–1497). The scene depicts the most notable personalities of the day, including Lorenzo the Magnificent and accurately records the costumes of the period.

The National Museum of the Bargello, housed in the Podesta Palace, contains a comprehensive collection of Italian decorative art and sculpture, including the composition of the Tuscan school of the 13th century, shown *left*, depicting 'Mary Magdalene'. **Michelangelo**'s superb tondo of the 'Madonna and Child' *right* is exhibited in the Chamber of the Council General, which is devoted to Donatello and other sculptors of the 15th century, whilst in the 13th Room, containing sculptures by Pollaiolo and Verrocchio, is Andrea del **Verrocchio**'s (c. 1435–1488) magnificent bronze statue of 'David' illustrated *overleaf*.

First published in Great Britain 1979 by Colour Library International Ltd.
© Illustrations: Foto Scala, Florence, Italy.
Colour separations by FERCROM, Barcelona, Spain.
Display and text filmsetting by Focus Photoset, London, England.
Printed and bound by SAGDOS - Brugherio (MI), Italy.
Published by Crescent Books, a division of Crown Publishers Inc.
Library of Congress Catalogue Card No. 78-59624
CRESCENT 1979